Sizable Savings for Free on Amazon.com

Get Crazy Discount Amazon Codes for FREE!

www.SizableSavings.com

by

Howie Arzt

INTRODUCTION

Learn How to Get Boatloads of Products on Amazon.com for Little or No Cost!

Shopping is expensive, but... it doesn't have to be!

I am going to reveal a simple method where you can purchase products on Amazon.com for pennies on the dollar (some products will even be Free!). Then you will learn about the one site that Amazon and EBay sellers don't want you to see!

CHAPTER 1

Boxes and More Boxes

The UPS man stops at my house every day and brings me several boxes. Some days, he needs to go back to his truck for a second or third trip because he can't carry them all at once. We know each other by name now because, one day, he asked me: "What is going on with all these boxes?" I shared this simple method with him, and now he is using it as well. Imagine... you get so many boxes from Amazon each and every day that you have the delivery people wondering!

Here's a small sampling:

Today, Matt (my UPS Man) came to my door with several boxes as usual, had a big smile on his face and said, "Check out these sunglasses I got for less than a dollar... saved $11.99"... Well, I have to tell you that made my day!!!

Some days, I get a few boxes, and some days, I get a whole load of boxes. Today, I think I got 7 or 8 and a few puffy envelopes. When I see them piling up, ready to be opened, all I can think is... Yay, I get to go open the presents! Every day is like a Holiday!

So... you're probably thinking... what's the catch? I don't blame you. I would think the same. Well, there is no catch, just some effort and a small amount of money. Also, a Prime Membership will be helpful but is not required. A Prime Membership will get you free shipping (as well as other benefits), if not there may be some small shipping charges. Shipping Charges can be eliminated by reaching Amazons minimum order amount where shipping does become free.

WARNING: This is a lot of fun and will become addictive!

There are products available from almost every category you can imagine. I have received kitchen utensils, kitchen gadgets, tools, toys, clothes, shoes, exercise equipment, musical instrument accessories, lamps, wallets, things I didn't even know existed... the list goes on and on! I've even purchased a half-size refrigerator! There is something for everyone.

So... Why would Amazon send you heavily discounted products?

Unless you've been hiding out in a cave for the past several years, I'm sure you know that Amazon.com has become the world's largest retailer. They have achieved this by allowing independent sellers to offer their products for sale on their website. These products pop up right alongside Amazon's products. There are thousands, maybe hundreds of thousands of sellers in the Amazon Marketplace, and they all want to get their products out to the world. Some are shipped directly from the sellers, but most are shipped to you directly from Amazon on their behalf.

Did you know there are several websites that exist for the sole purpose of assisting Amazon Sellers in building their business? They do this by offering products to you way below their cost, some even for free. I am about to share those websites with you and give you some tips on the best ways to use them. They are all free to join, no credit card needed.

CHAPTER 2

Getting Started

So, let's get right to it.

Simply visit these sites (there are 4 of them) and join for free as a "shopper." I'm not going to go into all the details because you will find them on each site. But, I will share some great tips on how to find the best products at the highest discounts.

Let's get you your first product. Simply visit:

1) www.SnagShout.com

This is the site that started me on this whole journey! It is very simple to use, and you will find many great products there.

They start by allowing you to "snag" (as they put it) one product every three days. As you continue to shop, they will add more snags to your account and allow you to purchase more products. At this time, I have 12 "snags" in my account, and they replenish them every 3 days.

Just go www.SnagShout.com and click on "Sign Up." Then read through their FAQ to see how it works.

After you join, you can start searching for a product. You can browse through the products on their main page or you can browse by category. You can also search for a specific product you may be looking for and see what comes up.

When you find a product that you would like, simply click on "Snag It." Then follow the steps to get your discount code and complete the purchase on Amazon. It's that simple! They will also send you your code by e-mail.

The best way to find the highest discounts on SnagShout is to

1) Choose a category

2) Sort by "Price: Biggest Saving %"

This will show you the highest discounts first. If you want to browse through all their products, just skip step 1 above and sort. As of this writing, the first 80 products are offered at 90% off or more... some even at 95% off! Every so often, you will see products pop up for FREE! You can also play around with the sorting and see what works best for you. If you check "Intimates," they will show you adult products as well.

CHAPTER 3

The Mother Load!

Now, let's increase your products... This next site lets you instantly get 20 codes / day up to 150 per month – I'm not kidding!

Visit:

2) www.Vipon.com

This is the site that really kicked it into high gear for me! It is my favorite of all the sites and where most of my crazy discounts have been found.

They have a ton of products, literally! You can spend hours just browsing through them (I know I have). If you love to shop, this site will be addicting!

Go to www.Vipon.com and, on the top left part of the site, click on "What Is Vipon" to see all the details. Then click on "Sign Up" and join as a "Shopper" for free. Once you create your membership, you can start looking for products.

At the top of the site, you will see the following links, which are self-explanatory:

Categories, Hot Deals, Instant Deals, Upcoming Deals, Editors' Picks

You can explore each of the above links and see what you find. The way to find the highest discounts on Vipon is to click on "Instant Deals" then, in the sort menu, choose "Price: Low to High." There is a choice that says, "Discount High to Low," but you will find higher discounts with the "Price" option.

As of this writing, the first product with the "Price" option is 99% Off. The "Discount" option is showing 90% off (still pretty good!). I have found the highest discounts by sorting by "Price."

Vipon allows you to search by category or to type a specific product into the search box. You can search for anything and see what you find. Each time you search for something, don't forget to sort. It will show you the highest discounts first.

I like to click on "Instant Deals," which allows you to get your code immediately.

You can browse through the products, and when you find one you would like, simply click on "Get Coupon." It will give you a coupon code then just go to Amazon and complete the purchase. Don't forget to enter your code during checkout... you will see the price reduce immediately.

When logged into your account, you can click on "My Deal Requests" to see your coupon codes. It is important that you purchase right away. Don't let the code get "stale." Sometimes, it will expire, and since the deals are so great, sometimes the sellers will put a limit on their codes either in total or per day. If you have a code, use it. When looking through "My Deal Requests," make sure to click on "already purchased," so they know you've purchased it.

Again, you can find anything on this site, including Adult Products if you are looking for them. If you don't want to see them, simply don't put a check in the category. They do have a separate category for Adult Products that you can browse through. Click on "Categories" to see the categories offered or click on "All Categories" to browse through everything. You never know what you will find, and the products are constantly changing. Every time I am looking for something specific, the first thing I do is go to Vipon, type it in the search box, and see if it comes up. Then I check the other sites mentioned in this book. Why pay retail??

CHAPTER 4

Key Word Suggestions

Here are some word suggestions to type in and search for. I have found many highly discounted and free products using these words. They can be searched for on every site mentioned in this book. Again, don't forget to sort if you want the highest discounts. I like to get 80% off or higher. Many products will come up at 50% off, which is still a great deal, but if you sort, you will save the most.

Suggested Search Terms

Leather	Electronic	Clock	Vegan
Phone	Cell	Automatic	Diet
Pen	Case	Video	Gourmet
Pencil	TV	Puzzle	Kids
Mirror	Kitchen	Pan	Blocks
Wallet	Gadget	Rechargeable	Toy
Game	Red	Natural	Binoculars
Chocolate	Blue	Camera	Magnifier
Vanilla	USB	Spy	Light
Candy	Office	Knife	Candle
Food	Sandals	Healthy	
Electric	Hat	Balloon	

The above should give you some great ideas to start... I'm sure you will think of many more.

CHAPTER 5

Ready for More?

Now... if Vipon doesn't tire you out and you're up for more shopping, visit:

3) www.JumpSend.com

This site has tons of products as well; however, it works a little differently than the first 2 sites. On JumpSend, you need to request a product and wait until the seller approves you for their discount code. This could happen right away, a few hours, a few days, or even a few months. Most are approved within hours or a day or two. You will receive an e-mail when a seller OK's your request, and you can see your codes under "Requested Deals" on their site. It is quite fun to keep checking back to see what you are approved for.

Go to www.JumpSend.com and go through the same process as the other sites to join free as a shopper.

You can request as many products as you want. To see the product on Amazon, click on the picture, and there will be a link that says, "See On Amazon.'

> ***Note***
> *I recommend viewing all products on Amazon, including those you find at the other sites. This way, you can see the full description and read the reviews. You can also make sure you are receiving the full discount stated. Sometimes, sellers play games by inflating the discount; most are honest though. All the sites will link to the products on Amazon.*

The coolest part of JumpSend is they have a sliding bar at the top of the site, which lets you set the discount amount you want to see. You can play around it and see what comes up. Set it between 90 and 100% to find the highest discounted products. Then you can go back and set it between 80 and 89, 70 and 79 etc. to check out the lower discounted products, or you can just slide it to 70 and 100% to see everything in that range. You can go through all of the products or 1 category at a time.

One thing to watch out for is sellers that are charging shipping. There have been items popping up that have shipping charges stated. I think they may be coming from the same seller. I usually avoid these, but you can decide for yourself if it is worth it. The items are still heavily discounted. I just don't like to pay for shipping. Guess I'm spoiled by now (-:

Don't sweat it if you don't get approved for every product you request. Some sellers are lazy, some disappear etc. It your product doesn't get approved eventually, it will show up as "Unavailable." Oh well – nothing lost, just keep requesting products. Sellers want you to purchase them because it increases their rankings on Amazon. As they get more sales (even if they don't profit), their listing ranks higher. They all want to be on page 1, not page 30+ where no one will see them.

CHAPTER 6

Check This One Out

Now, I will share one more site with you before I reveal the site that Amazon and EBay Sellers don't want you to see!

Check Out:

4) www.DealGoGoGo.com

There are a lot of great deals to be found here!

You join the same way as the others. Simply click on "Sign Up" and create a free membership. I also recommend reading their FAQ, which will give you more info. I don't want to say too much about this one because, every time I go there, their site is different. Despite all the changes, I have found some really crazy deals there!

Their search results are somewhat strange. You never know what is going to come up. For example, I just did a search on "pen." A lot of pens did come up but at pretty low discounts, certainly not what we're looking for. Then I clicked on "Filter" and sorted by "Highest Discount," and a lot of other products came up that were over 90% off but no pens?? This happens quite often.

I recommend checking it out. It will be well worth your time. Just like SnagShout and Vipon, the deals are instant, so you get your codes immediately. Currently, there is no limit on the amount of codes you can get, so shop away! Use the same methods I've shared in this book on DealGoGoGo, and you will find some awesome products at great discounts!

So… there you have it. Visit the above 4 sites and get crazy discounts!

CHAPTER 7

Examples

Here are some screenshots of actual purchases. You can see the discounts applied after the codes have been entered. This is just a sampling of what you will find. You can expect awesome deals like the ones below or even better:

Example 1

Example 2

3   Review items and shipping

(i) Want to save time on your next order and go directly to this step when checking out?
Check this box to save your delivery and billing preferences.

Guaranteed delivery date: Aug. 8, 2016 if you order in the next 6 hours and 49 minutes (Details)
Items shipped from Amazon.com

CC Boards Nonslip Bamboo Cutting Board: Wooden kitchen carving board with handle, groove for juice well and non slip rubber tabs; use for slicing cheese and bread or carving meat or a turkey!
$14.97 $1.00 √Prime
Qty: 1
Sold by: Saxeville Market LLC
$13.97 discount applied ▾

Add a gift receipt
and see other gift options

Ship in Amazon box

Choose your Prime delivery option:
○ Friday, Aug. 5
 $6.99 - One-Day Shipping
◉ Monday, Aug. 8
 FREE Two-Day Shipping
○ Wednesday, Aug. 10
 FREE Standard Shipping
○ Thursday, Aug. 11
 FREE No-Rush Shipping
 Get a $5.99 credit for Prime Pantry. Details

Place your order

By placing your order, you agree to Amazon.com's privacy notice and conditions of use.

Order Summary

Items:	$14.97
Shipping & handling:	$0.00
Promotion Applied:	-$13.97
Total before tax:	$1.00
Estimated tax to be collected:	$0.00
Total:	$1.00
Gift Card:	-$1.00
Order total:	**$0.00**

Qualifying offers:
- Promotion Applied

How are shipping costs calculated?

Prime shipping benefits have been applied to your order.

Place your order   **Order total: $0.00**
By placing your order, you agree to Amazon.com's privacy notice and conditions of use.

Example 3

Checkout (1 item)

1   Shipping address   Howie Arzt   Change

2   Payment method   Amazon.com Visa ending in   Change
Billing address.

▾ Add a gift card or promotion code
Enter code   Apply
✓ You successfully redeemed your promotional code

3   Review items and shipping

(i) Want to save time on your next order and go directly to this step when checking out?
Check this box to save your delivery and billing preferences.

Estimated delivery: Aug. 15, 2016
Items shipped from Amazon.com

Mato Lightweight Casual Hemp Backpack College School Laptop Shoulder Bohemian Boho Bag
$37.99 $2.00 √Prime & Free Returns
Details
Qty: 1

Choose your Prime delivery option:
○ 1 business day
 $3.99 - One-Day Shipping
◉ 2 business days
 FREE Two-Day Shipping
○ 4-5 business days

Place your order

By placing your order, you agree to Amazon.com's privacy notice and conditions of use.

Order Summary

Items:	$37.99
Shipping & handling:	$0.00
Promotion Applied:	-$35.99
Total before tax:	$2.00
Estimated tax to be collected:	$0.00
Order total:	**$2.00**

Qualifying offers:
- Promotion Applied

How are shipping costs calculated?

Prime shipping benefits have been applied to your order.

Example 4

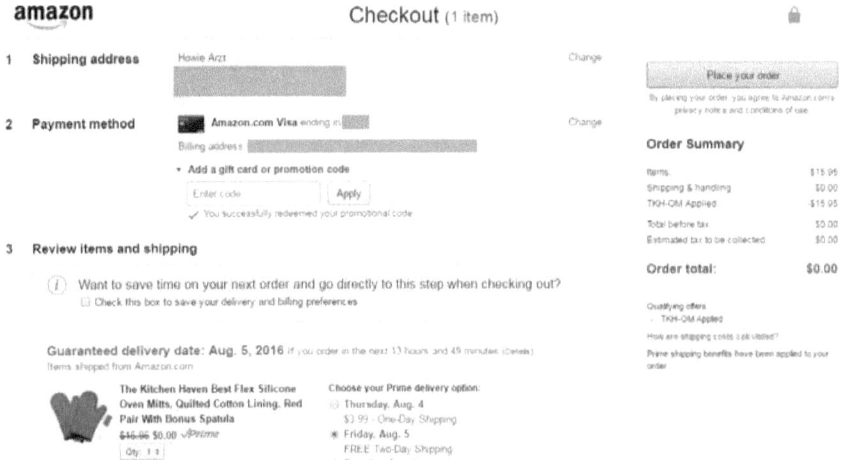

Example 5

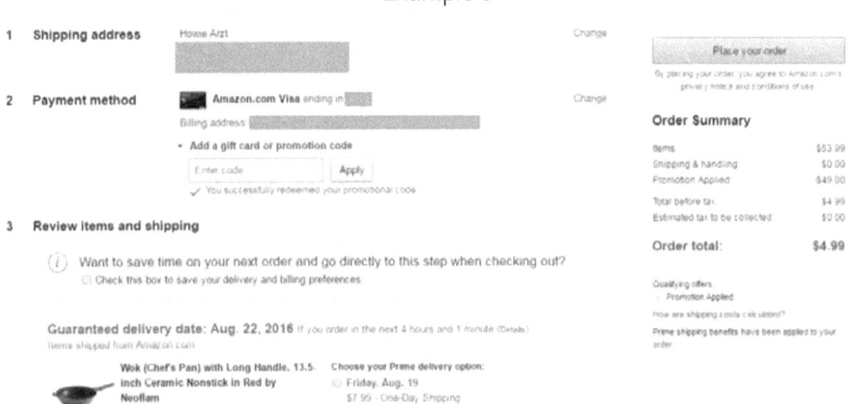

amazon

Checkout (1 item)

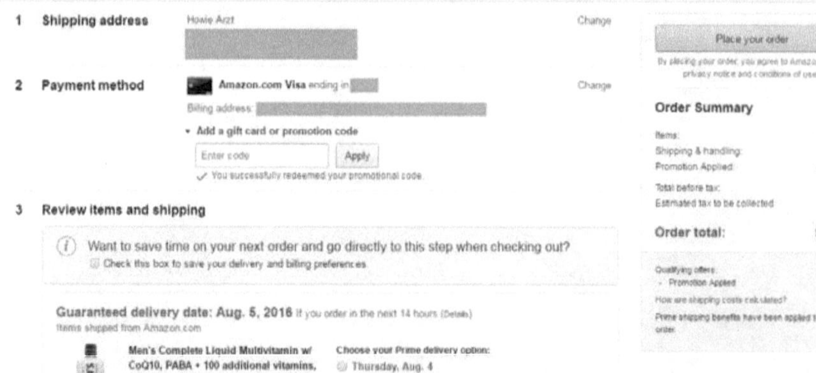

CHAPTER 8

Tips

Before you go shopping here are a few more tips…

1) Check the sites often. The products and discounts change all the time. New products are constantly added. On Vipon, they actually have a link for "Upcoming Deals" so you see ahead.

2) You will get e-mails from most of these sites showing you what is "hot" today. Sometimes, you will find a great deal on the e-mails, but the best discounts are found by searching through the sites.

3) Pay for it all with an Amazon Credit Card (if you can) and earn an additional 5% on the already ridiculously low prices. They give you 5% back as points in your Amazon account that can be directly applied at checkout.

4) If your coupon code doesn't work, sometimes all it takes is sending a simple e-mail to the seller. You will see a way to contact them in your members' area on each site. Most sellers will get back to you and send you a new code or take care of the issue. Of' course, there are some that just won't get back to you. When that happens… move on… there are lots more products available.

Here is a sample e-mail to send (an actual e-mail that was responded to quickly).

Tell the seller what happened, and in most cases, they will assist you.

5) In some cases, when you try to purchase the same product again in a different color / size / version, Amazon won't let you. They will tell you the code cannot be applied to this product. There is nothing you can do in this case except ask a relative or friend to purchase it for you through their account. Sometimes, Amazon will accept it.

6) If you make a mistake and don't get the discount, you can always cancel your order. For example: I clicked on "Place Order" before I clicked "Apply Code" on a $36.00 product that was discounted to $1.99. Due to my error, the order went through, and I was charged full price. I went into my account on Amazon, clicked on "My Orders" then on "Cancel Items" and followed their procedure to cancel. I then placed the order again, paid attention this time, and got the product for $1.99, which I was more than happy to pay (-:

7) If you don't remember if you purchased something (this happens when you receive so many products), visit the product on Amazon. If you've already purchased, you will see "You purchased this product on (date).

8) There are more sites popping up all the time like the ones I've shared. You can always search for them on your favorite search engine. I have found a few others that came and went but aren't

worth mentioning. But, I bet there are more good ones out there. The ones that I shared will keep you pretty busy, though!

9) Be creative when visiting these sites. I'm sure there are more ways to find great discounts that I haven't mentioned.

10) Think ahead of gifts you may need, birthdays, holidays etc. I Holiday Shop all year long. When I see something that would be a great gift for someone, I purchase it at a great discount and store it until needed.

11) Have Fun and Enjoy! This is very simple and is going to be a lot of fun. It does get addicting. It has for me!! (-:

CHAPTER 9

Bonus

BONUS
The One Site that Amazon and EBay Sellers Don't Want You to See!

So, we talked about the Amazon Marketplace, and we know almost any type of product can be purchased on EBay.

Where do you think all these products are coming from? The answer is simple... China of course! These days, almost everything is imported from China. Yes, there are things made in the USA and other countries around the world, but China has a tremendous export industry.

Are you familiar with "Drop shipping?" In a nutshell, Drop Shipping is when a product is sold and then shipped directly from the factory or warehouse to you on behalf of the seller. Example: You purchase a product from a seller on Amazon at retail price. The seller then orders the product at a wholesale price and has it shipped directly to you. The seller keeps the difference. This eliminates the need to purchase large amounts of products and keep inventory on hand. Also, the seller doesn't need to order the product until after they are paid. In most cases, the seller never even sees the product, and you think they have sent it to you.

Now, there are other ways that sellers on Amazon and EBay distribute their products, but many sellers are simply Drop Shipping. Well, what if you could purchase directly from the main source at wholesale prices?

Take a look at www.AliExpress.com

This is a huge marketplace, where factories in China offer their products for sale and will ship them directly to you, many with free shipping. You can search for anything there, and the prices are unbeatable!

The best way to get started with AliExpress is to go there and create an account (it's free) then watch the videos in the "New User Guide." To find the New User Guide, when on the "Sign Up" page, scroll down to the bottom, and under "Help" you will see it. This will explain everything to you.

Similar to the other sites, you can search for specific products or browse through categories. This is quite an amazing site with everything you can imagine and more!!

Since things are coming directly from China, it does take longer to receive your order. Many factories will ship their product by a method called "epacket," which they state takes 12 – 20 days, but many times, I have received them sooner. It is also costly to ship very large items, so for these, AliExpress doesn't make sense.

If you are not in a rush for an item, AliExpress is a great choice. Sometimes, I will search for an item I'm considering at a high discount on one of the other sites and will find it on AliExpress for even less.

CHAPTER 10

Conclusion

Thank you for purchasing and reading this book. I hope you have a lot of fun shopping with discounts and find many great products.

Please visit www.SizableSavings.com for more free coupons, information, and updates about discount shopping. Please share your finds and see what other readers have purchased. You will be able to post questions and help answer them as well.

Updates to this book will also be available there free of charge... or maybe with a code – LOL!

If you enjoyed this book, please leave a review on Amazon, so others can learn to save big, too.

I look forward to seeing you on www.SizableSavings.com.

Happy Shopping!

Howie Arzt

Shopping Addict / Author / Musician

ABOUT THE AUTHOR

Howie Arzt is a Stay At Home Non-Dad who loves to shop! He spent 25 years as a Band Teacher / Clarinet and Sax Player. He moved on from teaching and is now furthering his career as an Author and Public Speaker. He's created SizableSavings.com and is working on other projects, including DietEnd.com, where he is planning to share his experience getting healthy on a Keto / Low Carb High Fat Diet. He enjoys playing Clarinet and Saxophone and is one of the few men on this planet who absolutely loves to shop! He is happy to be able to share this great method of Discount Shopping.

www.ingramcontent.com/pod-product-compliance
Lightning Source LLC
Chambersburg PA
CBHW051240250726
48656CB00003B/1053